Bridge Pamphlet
No. 8

What I Saw

Laura Scott studied literature at university – she completed a Ph.D on the representation of inarticulate speech in Dickens' novels – but a few years later began writing poems, 'seriously, slowly and uncertainly'. She learned from Mimi Khalvati how to make poems 'out of thin air' and also to think of herself as a visual poet, writing poems about what she sees. Many of her poems come from the desire to make the reader 'see again with words something that doesn't reside in the words'. Teaching students at Norwich Art School, visual artists wanting to know how to use words, also helped her towards a poetry 'which is centrally, and simply, about looking at things'. Laura lives and works in Norwich.

What I Saw

LAURA SCOTT

RIALTO

ACKNOWLEDGEMENTS

Many thanks to the editors of the following journals, where several of these poems first appeared, *Edinburgh Review, Envoi, Magma, Poetry Review, Tate Etc,* and *The Rialto.*

BRIDGE PAMPHLETS

This is the eighth in a series of *The Rialto* pamphlets designed to cross the gap between magazine and book publication for new writers or, for established writers, that between collections. Previous pamphlets have been by Lorraine Mariner, Richard Lambert, Peter Sansom, Hannah Lowe, Jen Campbell and Luke Samuel Yates.

First published in 2013
The Rialto
PO Box 309 Aylsham Norwich
England NR11 6LN

ISBN 978-1-909632-01-1

The Publisher acknowledges financial assistance from Grants For Arts.

LOTTERY FUNDED

The Rialto is a Registered Charity No. 297553
Typeset in Berling 10 on 12.5pt
Design by Starfish, Norwich
Printed by Micropress Limited, Halesworth, Suffolk
Cover illustration by Laura Barnard

CONTENTS

OLD ROSE

I bring them into the house on a white day when the sea
has taken all the blue back to the waves and lie them
on their sides while I find the red vase with the pattern
of trees and bridges running around its base.
And then the yellow one slows me, shows me its petals
like parchment, so many crinkled together a foxglove
could creep in unnoticed and hide amongst them.
How did you get here, old rose, were you smuggled
through a chink in the years on to the walls of my garden?
Or dropped out of a window in a dark-panelled room
up above the river? You should be sung about or woven
into a conceit of thorns. You share the vase, here
on my desk with your younger sisters who hold their shape
and release their scent more prudently than you ever will.

THE BANKER'S DAUGHTER
Allan Ramsay 1759

As soon as he saw her he knew — he'd do her as
a half-length with a three quarters view of the head,
maybe a greeny grey behind her — that was how to coax

her face out of the doorway and into the room of his stare.
He liked the cut of her, the blunt edge of her jaw,
the cool way she looked back at him.

He'd get her to sit at one end of the sofa and watch her
arrange herself amongst her skirts and sleeves,
gathering her potential into the creases of her clothes

like a swan folding its wings back into their tips
as it settles on to the water. He'd wait for her to look up,
unguarded for a moment, so he got a flicker of the face

he wanted to paint before she pulled it back into the space
behind the eyes only practised sitters find. Later, when it
started to blur, he'd swill the image of her around in his head

like brandy warming in a glass. For now, he'd start with lines
— the slope of the sofa behind her to balance the tilt of her head,
the angle of her arms, down and out to the elbows,

back to the centre to meet on her lap. And finally the lines
of the black lace shawl framing the pleats of her bodice.
He'd paint the lace opening out into its pattern of loss

across her shoulder, the cinnabar pink of her dress behind it,
the froth of her cuffs, the soft folds of peach silk around
her throat. Only then would he start on the face,

building up layers of lead white to get the smoothness
of her forehead running back into the dark arc of her hair.
And as he waited for the thick paint to dry, he'd look

at what he'd done, pulsing as it set on to the canvas
and he'd find himself thinking of the goose egg he held as a boy,
the shudder in his fingers as they stretched around its shape,

the jolt in his stomach when he held it up to the candle
and he saw the blood vessels moving in the light,
and the heart beating right up against the shell.

THE ANNUNCIATION

The first time you looked and looked
until the other people shuffled away
to look at something else and it was just you
in front of the low square painting.
And what you saw was the swagger
in his eyes, as he looks up at her,
holding her in place with his stare.
And when I came and stood next to you,
you waited while I took in the lilies
and the olive tree, the fields and the river
behind him, before you took my eyes
in the palm of yours and led them
up to the curve of his and I saw it too.
More lover than angel, opening up the folds
of her glimpsed dress with his eyes, peeling back
her blue cloak with his outstretched hand - readying her
for the direct hit that started the whole thing off.
Years later, we went back a second time
but all that had gone. The swagger
had fallen away, like gilt peeling off an old frame
and we wondered what it was we'd seen.
This time the olive tree was starting
to look like a cross and his eyes were
as sad and as old as the hills behind him,
as if he saw the whole story reflected
back in the film of her eye.

AND THOSE WALLS CAME INTO OUR GAME

My mother took us to my godmother's flat with silver

      swords hanging on walls and silhouettes

of boys in uniforms - all high ceilinged Regency drawing room

      at the front

          damp maid's kitchen and bathroom at the back,

shabby like a Fortuny dress

      that has lost its pleats.

A flat in a town where houses were carved

      into flats and streets,

cut crescents of beige stone.

She let us go to the park on our own until we'd learned

      the shape of its banks and how to lean

          over the bridge and wait like children in a book

for the sounds of trains bursting into the light.

      She told us he'd be gone when we got back

and her words

      were bubbles in my drink, swimming up to my mouth.

HOME FARM

In the country parsley seeds itself.
Chickens peck out the eyes of the crows,
pin them on their backs
so they spread their black wings

like hands curling up to the sky.
Apples drag branches down
to the grass until the weight
of their juice breaks the bough

and they fall and wait for wasps.
Slats rot in the bench by the tennis court
and the man goes to the window
and shoots the crows. Their brothers

and sisters throw curses on his
bald head as he collects the dead
and ties their feet together
with string before he hangs them

on the chicken wire and their wings
fall open the wrong way
like black fans left in the field
of someone else's dream.

SOMEWHERE

I've always loved the bit when they're through
the gates but they haven't seen the Wizard yet,
when they're whisked off to be buffed and brushed.

The tin man is oiled and polished, the scarecrow
rolled and restuffed, like a plump cigarette,
the lion sits on a chair while they curl his mane

and file his claws, Dorothy has her hair brushed
and a red bow, even Toto gets clipped. I loved that
place, a pearl hanging on a necklace somewhere

between Oz and Kansas, where the flying monkeys
can't get us and our voices aren't breaking yet
with that cry of home rushing up our throats.

JULES ET JIM – THE TWO ACTORS

I wish you could see their faces, the dark-haired one
so full of intent, as if he were balancing an egg

on the spoon of his face. And the blond one, so different,
eyes nearly closed, his profile accidentally haloed

by something in the background so he looks like a saint
in a painting. It does what photos do, freezes people

mid-step, halts a lilting dance across the room,
as if one of the gods had clicked his fingers

to still a foot so it skims the floor forever, hovering,
pointing heel to toe, a ballet-dancer in black boots.

I wish you could see the shape the two of them make together,
off-centre, arms out, up and to the sides, an imperfect circle

running through their hands, while time leans against
the wall, and waits for them to finish their dance.

STARS

My son told me about the stars that died
        so long ago you can't imagine
which light still shines in the sky.

And I thought about the web that hangs
        across the corner of my window,
lines in circles, still moving in the wind

long after the spider has gone. Now I think
        of the ghosts that crowd the living,
pulling us towards them by our shirt lapels,

though we don't know whether they want
        to kiss us or hit us. And I think of you
telling me not to grieve for you too long.

IF I COULD SING

                    I'd bend the air
and make it sigh. I'd open my throat like a door

and my voice would flap its wings up to the beams
where the spiders listen to the dust. With one note,

I'll freeze their legs in mid thread. With another,
quieten the flies until they give themselves

like black and blue presents to the web. I'll wear a dress
the colour of pencil lead and people at the front

will hear it rustle as it pulls tight across my ribs
and my voice climbs higher and higher in its perfect legato

until the walls begin to pump around me like an accordion
swerving in and out of its chords. I'll melt the glass

back into sand and my voice will float out into the air,
running its fingers over the gull's feathers,

stroking the harp of grey barbs before it breaks their seal
and pulls them into oily strands so they fall like hawks

into the sea. Then I'll turn on a note and pour my voice
back into the room and wait for the applause,

the question on everyone's lips – what was that?

SOMETHING ABOUT BEING A PLANT WITHOUT ANY LIGHT

God knows precisely what she said.
I only heard bits of it and the door
was closed. Words came under it
like rats squeezing themselves
flat before they turned and went back
the other way. I pressed my ear
to the door but all I could hear was years
screaming themselves out of the walls,
pleading with her to be lived again.

COLLATERAL DAMAGE

At first you couldn't tell what it was
lying by the side of the road,

something they'd thrown from a car,
into the night. And then you saw

the slippers, calf-skin, dried hard
in the sun, the toe bit upturned

like the curve on the tip of a sledge
and shards of bone pushing out of them.

And then you had it, the taste of metal
on the tip of your tongue, and the smell

of petrol pushing your stomach
into your mouth. And you heard her

feet slipping on the rubble,
walking towards you, crying, pushing

her heart into her throat, calling him
back, beating her cheeks and tearing

her hair, like they used to when
they thought rain came from the stars.

TOLSTOY'S DOG

What is it about the lavender grey dog
        hanging around the men
playing with a piece of straw
        as if it were a stick
while Moscow burns behind them?
        What is it that makes her lie
across my mind as if she might be
        what all those words were about?

WHAT YOU LEFT OUT

The first time I heard it, its notes went through me
like milk through water, clouding into my bones
so I knew the end before it had even begun.

I sat and listened as you told me the story of the old man
and his three daughters, how he loved them all
but only one of them was good - the one who asked

for a rose instead of a dress, who talked of salt
instead of gold, who stood still and said nothing
while her sisters ran up and down flights of words.

And as the story drew itself around me, I saw her
sitting at a table, dragging her nail across the yolk,
rucking its film up into creases until it split

and the yellow pumped out into the white: that's when
it all went wrong, the beast threw back his head
and roared until the leaves shook on the trees,

the meat wouldn't cure, and the fish started to rot
as soon as they left the sea, the kingdom split
into a thousand pieces and blew back into the old man's eyes

like sand. And I waited for you to tell me about the mother -
how she loved this daughter best of all, how she stroked her hair
when she carried her back to the house at the end of the day.

BREATH

If I honoured you would you stay?
Would you hang around my ribs

smoothing ridges with your fingers
brushing them true again with your palm?

Would you billow sheets of muscle
red around my bones?

Would you soften the length of my spine,
teach my pulse to echo back your name?

I could take you under dark water
into the silence and wait for you to rush

in gulps of silver back to the surface.
I could kiss you back into my own throat.

DAUGHTER

A girl plays in the long grass under the tree
her hair cutting the air like a horse's tail

darting in and out of imagined rooms
finding paths through blades of green.

*

Skin white as rice cooked with lemon
left to cool on a blue plate in the sun

soft like suede under my hand
pulls me to her like a horse to water.

*

Her voice is thrown all over the house,
as if she were scattering seed into the earth

of every room as she runs past, or leaving
threads of herself to slow me as I walk by.

*

When you go away she sleeps in our bed,
fizzing like sherbert, waiting for me

to come back to her, unrecognisable,
her face still in sleep's hand.

*

In the last fold of the night, before the day
ruffles its feathers, I see her falling down the stairs

in someone else's house, the small of her back
hitting their cruel lines again and again.

Only dark red leaves left on the trees
the same colour as her hair

running down the back of her black coat
ahead of me this morning.

*

I watch her on a loop as she cartwheels
across the room with new precision

the softness lopped from her limbs as she goes,
a swoop of grief takes me in its arms.

*

I am like damp sand collapsing into itself
trying to remember the heel of a girl

now swimming in the sea. All I can do
is make lines for her to shimmer in.

AND THE SEA GOT INTO YOUR HAIR

To go to that house with its lino floors
and apple trees, blue and white sugar bowl
lying broken in pieces on the floor.

To have sugar like sand around your feet,
to feel the fear prickling up your calves,
to hear him shouting and find yourself

thrown out of your own throat while they
stand and watch - his face still angry, hers,
harder to read, turning away from you.

To be that child, with the garden behind you.
To sit on those trees nobody ever cut
and dip your feet in and out of the grass

while the branch moves up and down
like a horse under your weight.
To be that girl inside the white square

of the photograph, eyes squinting
in the sun, hair wet from the sea,
slicked into dark spikes around your neck.

OUR LADY OF AUGUST

High above the town on the apex of a golden triangle
she spreads her black wings into grey sky.

Clouds move like bad dreams around her.
Her body a trunk of stone. The sound of men singing

to each other, bragging so beautifully with the rain
running down their necks. If the wings could cut loose

they'd pull her up and up into the heavens above
the palazzos and fanned squares,

up to where the horses go in their heads
as they sweat and foam around the sanded square.

TURNER

His father saw it before anyone else,
the boy could paint light, could take the sky
into the bristles of his brush and lay it flat
like ribbon around a haberdasher's card.

He could take the curl of cloud, the line
of sea, and drop them on to canvas
pinned and waiting for him like a spider's
web on a window pane. He could make

colours his father had never seen appear
in white china bowls, grinding red lead
and smalt, madder and green slate
while his father washed bundles of hair

ready for the next day, rolling them
between finger and thumb, smoothing
the shafts flat as fish scales. In the morning,
when the light was at its sharpest, Joseph lit

the colour with water and gum, stirring in
honey so the Prussian blues and milky greens,
the scarlets and viridians, could breathe across
the hatched threads of the canvas. And while

his father knotted and threaded the hair
into silken caps, weaving it into clusters
of curls, the boy split shafts of light
until they shimmered on the tip of his brush.

And for a moment, the father looked up
from his work and was scared by the boy
who could paint God's light across the water,
the air's joy at being empty handed.

SEWING

Sew until the light has left the sky.
Sew until your arm has found its grace
up and to the side, up and to the side.

Sew until the nape of your neck softens
as you turn to look at the leaves falling
on the other side of the glass.

Look at them falling into the night.
Someone has been here before you
with a thread thicker and blacker than yours,

squeezing it flat between finger and thumb.
Sew until you see the folds of her years
pulled into place by your stitch.

POEMS

Maybe they're like fish
swimming inside you,
waiting for someone
to tap the glass.

FUNAMBULIST'S PRAYER

tightrope walk

Let me spread myself across the air
        like a fan of peacock's feathers,
shaking off the dust with my blues and greens.

Let me think of peaches and honey,
        of threads of red veining around the stone,
cutting the sweet yellow flesh in half.

Let me find the line's balance under my foot
        like that church we found in the v
of the road, with its garden at the front where trees

curled like vines and cars roared past on either side
        like they do in black and white films.
Let me draw the stillness from the wall in through

my fingertips until it runs through the rays of my feet.
        Let me find the air's ease as I remember
how, up here, grace hides her face in difficulty's sleeve.